AVATAR

The Official Cookbook of Pandora

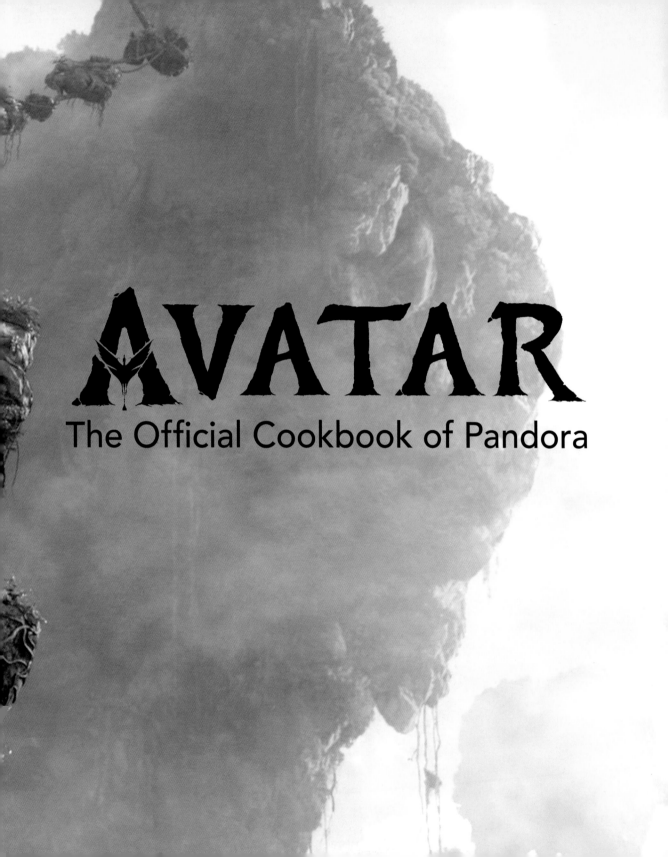

AVATAR
The Official Cookbook of Pandora

CONTENTS

1 Omatikaya Offerings

Pandora's bounty is all around in the lush forests that the Omatikaya call home. Nourishing and energy-giving, these recipes take you from foraged fruit oatmeal to woodland mushroom ramen, bringing the spirit of the forest to family meals.

OVUMSHROOM BURGER

The damp rainforests of Pandora provide the Na'vi with plenty of fungi. This burger celebrates all the colors of the forest canopy, bringing together marinated mushrooms with a garnish of pickled red cabbage, topped with a chive and mustard mayo.

Serves 4

**Prep 10 mins plus marinating
Cook 35 mins**

8 Portobello mushrooms
4 vegan brioche buns
sunflower oil, for brushing
1 head of Little Gem lettuce

For the marinade
2 tbsp soy sauce
1 tsp maple syrup
2 tsp rice wine vinegar
1 garlic clove, minced

For the pickled red cabbage
¼ red cabbage, thinly sliced
freshly squeezed juice of ½ lime
¼ tsp garlic salt

For the mustard mayo
1 tbsp American mustard
4 tbsp vegan mayonnaise
1 tbsp finely snipped chives

1 Combine the ingredients for the marinade in a large shallow dish, add the mushrooms, and leave to marinate for 1 hour at room temperature.

2 While the mushrooms are marinating, prepare the other elements. Combine the thinly sliced cabbage with the lime juice, season with garlic salt, and give a good stir. Set aside.

3 For the mustard mayo, simply combine all the ingredients in a small bowl and set aside.

4 Heat a ridged cast-iron grill pan until smoking hot and lightly toast the buns on each side, taking care not to burn them. Set aside.

5 To cook the mushrooms, drain off any excess marinade on a paper towel, then brush each mushroom with oil. Grill two at time for about 4–5 minutes each side until tender, turning halfway through cooking. Brush with any remaining marinade.

6 To assemble the burgers, generously spread mustard mayo over the base of each bun; top with lettuce and two grilled mushrooms per burger. Finish with the pickled red cabbage and bun lid.

TACO SURPRISE

Tacos always bring everyone together around the table. These family favorites are filled with a rainbow-colored slaw and topped with a forest surprise—chili crispy bugs! Nutritious and high in protein, they'll soon become your go-to snack.

Makes 8

Prep 15 mins
Cook 5 mins plus marinating

8 soft shell tacos
2/3 cup (125g) canned black beans,
 drained and rinsed
1 ripe avocado, diced
¼ cup (50g) edible chili insects
 or crispy fried onions
1 small red chili, seeded
 and sliced
sour cream to serve

For the rainbow slaw
¼ small red cabbage, finely
 shredded (about 7oz/200g)
1 small yellow bell pepper, sliced
8 radishes, sliced into thin rounds
2 green onions, thinly sliced
handful of chopped cilantro,
 plus extra to garnish
freshly squeezed juice and zest
 of 1 lime
pinch of garlic salt

1 Preheat the oven to 350ºF (180ºC).

2 To make the rainbow slaw, combine the shredded cabbage, sliced bell pepper, radishes, green onions, and cilantro in a large bowl. Add the lime zest and juice, and season with the garlic salt. Put to one side to marinate for 10 minutes.

3 Warm the soft taco shells in the oven for 3 minutes. To build the tacos, fill each shell with some of the slaw, and top with black beans, avocado, and crispy chili bugs or fried onions. Scatter with cilantro and sliced chili, and serve with sour cream on the side.

FORAGED FRUITS BREAKFAST

Transport yourself to the forest and a morning spent foraging for fresh fruit in order to create this bowl of creamy oats topped with fresh raspberries and chopped pistachios. You can substitute or mix in other berries, depending on what nature has to offer.

Serves 2

Prep 5 mins
Cook 10 mins

1¾ cups (150g) rolled oats
1¼ cups (300ml) almond milk,
   or milk of your choice
1 tbsp ground flaxseeds
3 tbsp chopped unsalted pistachios

To serve
2 tbsp raspberry preserve
handful of fresh raspberries
honey

1 Put the oats, almond milk, and ½ cup (100ml) water in a saucepan and cook over low heat for about 5–6 minutes, stirring gently.

2 Mix through the flaxseeds and half the pistachios and divide the oatmeal between two serving bowls. Top with a swirl of raspberry preserve, some fresh raspberries, the remaining pistachios, and a drizzle of honey.

RAINFOREST SOURDOUGH TOAST

When it's time to refuel, these toasted open sandwiches topped with maple halloumi and avocado will hit the spot. They are perfect for feeding hungry mouths after an adventure in the forest.

Serves 2

Prep 10 mins
Cook 15 mins

2 thick slices of sourdough
olive oil, for drizzling
1 garlic clove
3½oz (100g) halloumi, cut into
   6 slices
1 tbsp maple syrup
pinch of crushed red pepper
   flakes
1 avocado
1 red chili, seeded and
   sliced
zest of ½ lemon
a few mint leaves, shredded
freshly ground black pepper

1 Heat a ridged cast-iron grill pan to smoking hot and toast the bread for 2–3 minutes on each side until lightly toasted.

2 Drizzle each slice of toast with a little olive oil, cut the garlic clove in half, and rub it over the toast.

3 Grill the halloumi slices in the ridged pan until crisp, about 2–3 minutes each side. Remove from the pan and brush with the maple syrup, then sprinkle with red pepper flakes. Divide the halloumi between the toast slices.

4 Peel and halve the avocado and cut thin slices into each avocado half, leaving the top ¾in (2cm) intact. Lightly press down with the palm of your hand to create a fan shape. Top each toast with a fan of avocado. Season with pepper and garnish with lemon zest, chili, and a sprinkling of shredded mint.

WOODLAND MUSHROOM RAMEN

This fragrant mushroom broth brings all the bounty of the woodland floor together in harmony in one bowl. For a vegan version, replace the egg with silken tofu.

Serves 2

Prep 10 mins
Cook 1 hour

1 egg
4½oz (125g) dried ramen noodles
5½oz (150g) mixed mushrooms,
   large ones sliced
2 baby bok choy
1 carrot, peeled and cut into julienne

For the broth
1½oz (40g) dried mushrooms
1 tbsp grated fresh ginger root
2 large garlic cloves, minced
2 tbsp miso paste
2 tbsp soy sauce
2 whole green onions

To serve
toasted sesame seeds
2 green onions, sliced
chili oil

1 For the broth, blend the dried mushrooms to a fine powder using a food processor or pestle and mortar.

2 Add the ginger and garlic to a large pan with the miso paste and soy sauce, along with two whole green onions. Pour over 6¼ cups (1.5 litres) boiled water, and bring to a simmer. Continue to simmer for 45 minutes without a lid.

3 While the broth is cooking, bring a pan of water to a boil and add the egg. Boil for 7 minutes, then remove with a slotted spoon and plunge into cold water. Peel the cooled egg and set aside.

4 Add the ramen noodles to the pan of boiling water and cook following the package instructions. Drain and divide between two serving bowls.

5 Discard the whole green onions from the broth and add the mushrooms and bok choy. Simmer for 3–4 minutes.

6 Strain out the vegetables from the broth and divide between the bowls. Ladle the broth over each bowl. Halve the egg and add a half to each bowl. Sprinkle each serving with sesame seeds and sliced green onions, and serve with a drizzle of chili oil.

GREEN SHAKSHUKA

For this satisfying breakfast dish, spinach and herbs replace the traditional tomatoes to provide a spiced green bed for baked eggs, topped with crispy halloumi and a harissa and yogurt dressing.

Serves 4

Prep 10 mins
Cook 30 mins

1oz (30g) flat-leaf parsley
1oz (30g) cilantro
3oz (80g) baby spinach
1 tbsp Dijon mustard
2 tbsp capers
2 garlic cloves, sliced
½ cup (100ml) vegetable stock
3 tbsp olive oil
1 large onion, chopped
1 large green bell pepper, diced
1 jalapeño pepper, seeded and sliced
½ tsp cumin seeds
½ tsp ground cilantro
4 eggs
3oz (80g) halloumi, cut into small chunks
1 tbsp harissa paste
3 tbsp Greek-style yogurt
handful of pea shoots, to garnish
crusty bread, to serve
sea salt and freshly ground black pepper

10in (26cm) oven-safe skillet

1 In a food processor, blend the herbs and half the spinach with the mustard, capers, garlic, stock, and 2 tablespoons of olive oil to form a smooth sauce. Set aside.

2 Preheat the oven to 350°F/180°C. Heat the remaining tablespoon of olive oil in an oven-safe skillet over medium heat. Add the onion, pepper, garlic, jalapeño pepper, spices, and a pinch of salt. Cook for 5–7 minutes, or until softened.

3 Pour the blended sauce into the pan and gently simmer for 5 minutes before adding the remaining spinach. Cook until the spinach has wilted, then remove the pan from the heat.

4 Make a well in the sauce using the back of a spoon and crack an egg into the well. Repeat with the remaining eggs and season.

5 Place the skillet in the oven and bake for 8–10 minutes, or until the eggs are cooked to your liking.

6 While the dish is baking, fry the halloumi in a dry pan until crisp and golden. Mix the harissa and yogurt together in a serving bowl.

7 Remove the pan from the oven and garnish with the halloumi and pea shoots. Serve warm with crusty bread and harissa yogurt on the side.

HARMONY SALAD

Bright and refreshing, this salad balances the sweetness
of watermelon with creamy feta and a topping of crunchy,
maple-toasted seeds.

Serves 4

Prep 10 mins
Cook 10 mins

3½oz (100g) arugula leaves
2¼lb (1kg) watermelon, cut into
   bite-sized cubes
handful of roughly chopped mint
5½oz (150g) feta cheese
2 green onions, sliced
crusty bread, to serve
sea salt

For the maple-toasted seeds
6 tbsp mixed seeds, such as
   pumpkin, sunflower, flaxseeds
2 tsp maple syrup
pinch of crushed red pepper
   flakes, optional

For the dressing
3 tbsp extra-virgin olive oil
2 tbsp balsamic vinegar
zest and freshly squeezed juice of
   ½ lemon

1 Toast the seeds in a small, dry frying pan over medium heat for
about 4 minutes. Drizzle over the maple syrup and remove from
the heat. Add a pinch of salt and chili flakes, if using, then transfer
to a small bowl to cool.

2 Dress a serving platter with the argula leaves. In a large bowl,
whisk together the oil, vinegar, and lemon juice and zest, and
season to taste.

3 Toss the melon and half the chopped mint in the dressing, then
layer over the arugula leaves. Top with crumbled feta and green
onions, and scatter over the remaining mint leaves and toasted
seeds. Serve with some crusty bread.

PARADISE COCKTAIL

A perfect party cocktail that captures the swirling, elemental colors of the Pandoran skies. Exotic passion fruit and banana rum form the base, with the extra surprise of bubble tea pearls.

Serves 2

Prep 10 mins

ice
1.7fl oz (50ml) vodka
1.7fl oz (50ml) blue curaçao
2 passion fruit
2 tbsp passion fruit boba (bubble tea pearls)
1.7fl oz (50ml) banana rum
¼ cup (50ml) freshly squeezed lime juice
¼ cup (50ml) passion fruit juice
mint sprigs, to garnish

Cocktail shaker

1 Fill two high-ball glasses with ice. Add a handful of ice to a cocktail shaker and pour over the vodka and blue curaçao. Shake vigorously for 30 seconds, then strain between the glasses.

2 Halve one fresh passion fruit and divide the seeds between the glasses. Add a tablespoon of boba pearls to each glass.

3 Rinse out the shaker and add more ice. Shake up the banana rum, lime juice, and passion fruit juice. Slowly pour between each glass, taking care not to disturb the lower layer too much. Garnish with a sprig of mint and a slice of passion fruit.

BOTANIST'S LUNCH BOWL

This multicolored buddha bowl is inspired by the xenobotanists at Biolab, bringing together planet-friendly ingredients that nurture and sustain. A base of quinoa and lemon kale is topped with avocado, black beans, and carrot strips. Finish with smoky red bell pepper sauce, with cashews for crunch.

Serves 2

Prep 10 mins
Cook 10 mins

9oz (250g) package of mixed quinoa
2oz (60g) kale, shredded
zest and freshly squeezed juice of
  1 lemon
sesame oil
1 avocado, peeled, halved, and sliced
1 carrot, cut into julienne
3½oz (100g) canned black beans,
  drained and rinsed
4 tbsp toasted cashew nuts,
  chopped
1 roasted red bell pepper
  (5½oz/150g)
1 tbsp chipotle sauce
small handful of cilantro
sea salt

1 Heat the quinoa following the package instructions and divide between two serving bowls.

2 In a large bowl, toss together the kale with the lemon zest, half the lemon juice, and a pinch of salt. Crumple together between your hands, then drizzle with sesame oil and divide between the serving bowls along with a fan of sliced avocado, a nest of carrot strips, and the black beans.

3 In a blender, grind 3 tablespoons of cashew nuts to a fine powder, then add the red bell pepper, chipotle sauce, and remaining lemon juice. Blend until smooth, then add to each bowl, finishing with the remaining chopped cashews and a sprinkle of cilantro leaves.

HUNTERS' TRAIL MIX

The forest clan of the Omatikaya have a deep-rooted connection to their environment, only taking what they need and honoring the bounty of the jungle. This trail mix of nuts and seeds is ideal for boosting hunters' energy levels.

Serves 6–8 as a snack

Prep 5 mins
Cook 20 mins plus cooling

1–1½ cups (150g) almonds or
    pecans
1 cup (150g) cashews
¾ cup (100g) pumpkin seeds
3 tbsp coconut oil, melted
2 tbsp brown rice syrup
1 tbsp chia seeds
¾ cup (60g) coconut flakes
1 tsp ground cinnamon
¼ cup (50g) red raisins
¼ cup (50g) blue-coated chocolate
    candies

1 Preheat the oven to 375ºF (190ºC) and line a large baking sheet with parchment paper. Add the nuts and pumpkin seeds, pour over the coconut oil and rice syrup, and stir to coat everything. Bake in the oven for 10–15 minutes.

2 Remove the nuts from the oven and add the chia seeds, coconut flakes, and cinnamon. Stir again to combine and bake for 5 more minutes until everything is light and golden.

3 Remove the trail mix from the oven and leave to cool completely before mixing through the raisins and candy. Transfer to an airtight container and store for up to 1 month.

HALLELUJAH MOUNTAIN CUPS

With a chewy core of magma-colored raspberry beneath a salty dark chocolate topping, these tangy cups are bite-sized bursts of pure Pandoran energy.

Makes 12

**Prep 20 mins plus freezing
Cook 5 mins**

For the base
1 tsp vanilla extract
¼ cup (25g) shredded coconut
1 tbsp cocoa powder
1½oz (40g) whole almonds
   (about a handful)
5 medjool dates

For the raspberry filling
3½oz (100g) frozen raspberries
¼ cup (20g) shredded coconut
2 tsp maple syrup

3oz (80g) dark chocolate (70–80%
   cocoa solids), chopped
1 tbsp coconut oil
1 tsp sea salt flakes

**12-cup mini muffin tin lined with
mini muffin cup liners**

1 Put the ingredients for the base into a food processor and blend until they come together into a sticky dough. Divide between the muffin cups and press down with your thumb to make a base layer.

2 Add the ingredients for the raspberry filling to the food processor and blend for a few seconds to combine. Spoon the mixture on top of the base. Transfer the muffin tin to the freezer for 15 minutes to firm up.

3 Melt the dark chocolate and coconut oil together, either in a heat-resistant bowl set over a pan of gently simmering water, taking care not to let the bowl touch the water, or in short bursts in the microwave, taking care not to let the chocolate get too hot.

4 Remove the muffin tin from the freezer and top each cup with a couple of spoons of the melted chocolate and a pinch of sea salt flakes. Store in the freezer for up to a week. Let sit at room temperature for 5–10 minutes before serving.

2

RDA Rations

While the RDA establishes a new base for the human race on Pandora, they serve up familiar foods with a vegan twist to respect their world's limited resources. Here, you'll find reimagined mac 'n' cheese, burgers, and comforting stews to sustain any expedition.

HELL'S GATE CORNBREAD MUFFINS

These sweet, moist cornbread muffins with a kick of jalapeños are perfect for sharing with the crew on expeditions or serving alongside a campfire stew.

Makes 12

Prep 5 mins
Cook 45 mins

2 tbsp ground flaxseeds
4 tbsp sparkling water
1¼ cups (150g) all-purpose flour
1 cup (170g) cornmeal
1 tbsp baking powder
¼ tsp sea salt
⅓ cup (80ml) sunflower oil
1 cup (250ml) soy milk or plant-based alternative
¼ cup (130g) frozen sweetcorn
2 jalapeño peppers, seeded and thinly sliced

12-cup muffin tin lined with muffin cup liners

1 Preheat the oven to 400ºF (200ºC). Whisk together the flaxseeds and water and set aside for 5 minutes.

2 Add the remaining dry ingredients to a large bowl, pour over the oil and soy milk, then add the flaxseed mix. Using a spatula, gently fold together to form a smooth batter. Stir through the corn and the sliced jalapeños, reserving a few slices for topping.

3 Divide the mixture between the muffin cups and top each with a few slices of jalapeño. Bake in the center of the oven for 30–35 minutes until risen and golden. Serve warm with non-dairy spread or butter.

SUPERCHARGED STEAK

Roasted red cabbage makes a planet-friendly stand-in for classic steak. Ramp up the flavors with a sweet-and-sour topping of pomegranate molasses, served on a bed of cannellini beans and roasted tomatoes.

Serves 4

Prep 10 mins
Cook 40 mins

1 large red cabbage, cut into 2½in (6cm) thick wedges
½ tsp ground cumin
1½ tsp smoked paprika
2 tbsp olive oil
2 tbsp pomegranate molasses
14oz (400g) can cannellini beans, drained and rinsed
8 cherry tomatoes, halved
small handful of chopped mint
small handful of chopped flat-leaf parsley
4 tbsp pomegranate seeds
2 tbsp pine nuts, toasted
sea salt

1 Preheat the oven to 400ºF (200ºC). Line a baking sheet with parchment paper and space the cabbage steaks out on the sheet.

2 Mix the spices with a pinch of salt and 1 tablespoon of olive oil, and brush over the cabbage, coating both sides. Roast in the oven for 25 minutes.

3 Remove the sheet from the oven and brush the cabbage steaks with some of the pomegranate molasses, carefully turn the steaks, and brush the other side. Scatter over the cannellini beans, cherry tomatoes, and half the herbs, and drizzle with the remaining olive oil. Return to the oven for 10–15 more minutes, until the cabbage is cooked through and lightly charred.

4 Divide the cannellini beans and tomatoes between serving plates; top each serving with a cabbage steak; scatter with pomegranate seeds, pine nuts, and the remaining chopped herbs.

BRIDGEHEAD CITY BURGER

Any construction worker at Bridgehead City would be pleased to dig into this home-away-from-home burger. This vegan version combines pulled jackfruit with a barbecue sauce, served with a side order of sweet potato fries.

Serves 4

Prep 10 mins
Cook 25 mins

9oz (240g) canned jackfruit, rinsed and drained
2 tbsp barbecue sauce
2 large sweet potatoes, unpeeled, cut into thin fries
1 tbsp sunflower oil
4 whole-wheat vegan buns
4 tbsp vegan mayonnaise
4 small handfuls of mixed salad leaves
2 tbsp crispy fried onions
1 beefsteak tomato, sliced into 4 slices
1 small red onion, sliced into rings
sea salt

1 Preheat the oven to 400°F (200°C).

2 Place the jackfruit in a bowl and shred it with a fork. Add the barbecue sauce and stir to coat. Line a baking sheet with foil. Spread the jackfruit out in a single layer and bake for 15–20 minutes, until crisped up at the edges and heated through.

3 Meanwhile, spread the sweet potato fries out onto a separate lined baking sheet, drizzle with 1 tablespoon of oil and a sprinkle of salt. Roast for 15–20 minutes until starting to brown, turning halfway through.

4 Split the buns and lightly toast both sides in a warm pan. To build the burger, spread a little mayonnaise on the base of each bun, then top with a handful of salad leaves and a quarter of the jackfruit. Sprinkle with crispy fried onions and add a tomato slice and a few onion rings. Top with the bun lid and serve with the sweet potato fries.

UNOBTANIUM ENERGY BITES

Channel the super-conducting properties of unobtanium with these bite-sized nuggets that contain blue spirulina, dates, oats, and nut butter, rolled in vitamin-rich sunflower seeds.

Makes 16

Prep 15 mins

2 tbsp sunflower seeds
1½ tbsp blue spirulina powder
6 medjool dates
6 tbsp nut butter, such as cashew or
   almond
8 tbsp rolled oats
½ tsp vanilla extract
2 tsp brown rice syrup
pinch of pink sea salt

1 In a food processor, grind the sunflower seeds to a rough crumb, then set aside in a shallow bowl.

2 Add the remaining ingredients to the blender and process into a soft dough. Make sure the mix comes together and is moist but not wet.

3 Roll pieces of the mixture between your palms into balls a little bigger than a teaspoon in size, then roll each ball in the sunflower seed crumbs to coat it all over.

4 Chill the coated balls in the refrigerator for 1 hour before serving. Store in an airtight container for up to a week.

WARRIOR "WINGS"

These crispy, battered cauliflower "wings" are smothered in a
Cajun lime glaze, making them irresistible finger food to serve
as part of a vegan feast.

Serves 4

Prep 15 mins
Cook 55 mins

1 cup (150g) all-purpose flour
1 tsp smoked paprika
1 tsp onion powder
1 tsp garlic powder
1 tsp fine sea salt
1 tsp apple cider vinegar
1 cup (250ml) almond milk
1 head of cauliflower (about
    2lb/900g), cut into bite-sized
    florets
2 tbsp sunflower oil
small bunch of chives, snipped
vegan mayonnaise, to serve

For the Cajun glaze
1 tbsp maple syrup
freshly squeezed juice and zest of
    1 lime
1 tsp Cajun seasoning

1 Preheat the oven to 400ºF (200ºC). Line two large baking sheets
with parchment paper and drizzle with 1 tbsp of sunflower oil.

2 In a bowl, combine the flour, spices, and salt. Add the vinegar and
remaining sunflower oil to the almond milk and pour over the dry
mix, whisking together to make a smooth batter.

3 Dip the cauliflower florets one by one into the batter and roll to
coat, using a spoon to scoop the batter into all the nooks and
crannies. Space the florets out on the baking sheets, ensuring they
are not overcrowded.

4 Bake for 20 minutes, turn each floret, and bake for 20–25 more
minutes, or until crisp and golden.

5 Gently warm the ingredients for the Cajun glaze in a small pan for
2–3 minutes, until just starting to bubble. Use a pastry brush to
coat each of the cauliflower wings in the sticky sauce.

6 Transfer the coated wings to a serving platter, sprinkle with half the
chives, and stir the remaining chives through a small bowl of vegan
mayonnaise for dipping.

RDA CORN RIBS

Perfect on their own or served alongside a burger and "wings"
(see pages 50 and 56), these roasted corn ribs are accompanied
by a chili and lime ranch sauce.

Serves 4–6

Prep 15 mins
Cook 30 mins

4 corn on the cob
1 tbsp olive oil
freshly squeezed juice and zest of
   1 lime
1 tsp hot smoked paprika
1 tsp soft brown sugar
sea salt and freshly ground black
   pepper

For the ranch sauce
½ cup (125ml) plain coconut
   or plant-based yogurt
½ tsp apple cider vinegar
½ tsp chopped dill
½ tsp onion powder
¼ tsp fine sea salt
pinch of smoked paprika
freshly ground black pepper

1 Make the ranch sauce. In a bowl, combine the yogurt, vinegar, dill, onion powder, salt, paprika, and a grind of black pepper. Mix to combine, then spoon into a serving bowl.

2 Preheat the oven to 400°F (200°C). Line two large baking sheets with parchment paper.

3 To cut the corn into ribs, stand each cob vertically on a chopping board. Use a large, sharp knife and a rocking motion through the top to carefully cut down through the center. Then repeat, using the same technique, to cut each slice in half again down the length, so you are left with quarters from each cob.

4 In a bowl, mix together the oil, lime juice, paprika, sugar, and a pinch of salt. Brush this over the ribs of corn so that all the kernels are coated.

5 Divide the ribs between the lined baking sheets, spacing them well apart, and bake for 25–30 minutes, turning halfway. The corn is ready when lightly charred and slightly curled up.

6 Transfer the ribs to a serving bowl and scatter with the lime zest. Serve with the ranch sauce on the side for dipping.

FRONTIER PANCAKES

This fluffy pile of vegan pancakes served with blueberry syrup is like a taste of home for the hundreds of RDA operatives who make the interstellar journey from Earth to Pandora.

Serves 4

Prep 10 mins
Cook 20 mins

2 cups (240g) all-purpose flour
1 tbsp baking powder
2 tbsp cornflour
1½ cups (330ml) dairy-free
  or plant-based milk
1 tsp maple syrup
2 tsp apple cider vinegar
1 large banana, sliced, to serve

For the blueberry syrup
4½oz about 1 cup (125g) blueberries
3 tbsp maple syrup

1 To make the blueberry syrup, add the blueberries to a small pan along with the maple syrup and 2 tablespoons water. Bring to a simmer for 5 minutes, stirring to burst the blueberries. Pour into a jug or bowl ready to serve.

2 Preheat the oven to 275ºF (140ºC). Sift the flour, baking powder, and cornflour into a large bowl. In a separate bowl or jug, lightly whisk together the milk, maple syrup, and vinegar. Add to the dry ingredients and, using a fork, beat together until you have a smooth batter.

3 Heat a dry, nonstick frying pan on low heat. Ladle about 3 tablespoons of batter onto the hot pan and cook for 20–30 seconds (or when bubbles start to form on top) before carefully flipping onto the other side. Cook for 20–30 more seconds. Transfer to a baking sheet and keep warm in the oven while you repeat with the remaining batter to make a total of 12 pancakes.

4 Serve stacks of 3 pancakes per person, topped with banana slices. Pour over the blueberry syrup to finish.

COMMAND CENTER CHIPS AND DIP

Gather everyone together around a bowl of harissa-flavored sweet potato chips and herby tahini dip. Perfect for team bonding. You can substitute the harissa with red pesto to dial down the heat.

Serves 8–10

Prep 10 mins
Cook 40–45 mins

3 large sweet potatoes, unpeeled
3 tbsp olive oil
1 tbsp harissa, chili paste, or
  red pesto
½ tsp garlic sea salt
2 sprigs of lemon thyme, leaves
  picked
2 tbsp pomegranate molasses

For the tahini dip
6 tbsp tahini
freshly squeezed juice and zest of
  ½ lemon
small handful of mixed herbs such as
  mint, flat-leaf parsley, and dill

1   Preheat the oven to 220ºC/200ºC fan/425ºF/Gas 7. Line two baking sheets with parchment paper.

2   Slice the sweet potatoes into thin rounds, about ⅛in (3mm) thick and add to a large ziplock bag along with the olive oil, harissa, garlic salt, and thyme leaves. Seal the bag and shake vigorously until the sweet potatoes are well-coated.

3   Divide the sweet potatoes between the baking sheets, ensuring that they are not overcrowded, and cook for 35–40 minutes, turning occasionally, until lightly brown. Drizzle with the pomegranate molasses and return to the oven for 5 minutes.

4   While the chips are cooking, make the tahini dip. Combine the tahini, lemon zest and juice, and ⅓ cup (80ml) water, stirring until smooth. Add a splash more water if it is too thick.

5   Roll the herbs into a tight bundle and finely chop. Stir into the dip, season to taste, and spoon into a serving bowl. Serve the chips with the dip on the side.

SKIPPER'S STEW

A hearty dish to satisfy any appetite brought on by the sea air, this smoky bean stew is given extra richness from roasted mushrooms stirred through at the end. Gather your crew and dig in!

Serves 6

Prep 10 mins
Cook 35 mins

2 tbsp olive oil
12 shallots, peeled
1 tbsp tomato paste
2 tbsp smoked paprika
1 tsp cumin seeds
2 bay leaves
2 x 14oz (400g) cans plum tomatoes
1 tbsp maple syrup
1 tbsp red wine vinegar
14oz (400g) can lima beans, drained and rinsed
14oz (400g) can cranberry beans, drained and rinsed
14oz (400g) can navy beans, drained and rinsed
4 fat garlic cloves, crushed
1 tbsp mushroom ketchup, tamari, or soy sauce
1lb 2oz (500g) chestnut mushrooms, whole
2 sprigs of thyme
small handful of chopped flat-leaf parsley
Hell's Gate Cornbread Muffins, see page 44, to serve
sea salt and freshly ground black pepper

1 Add 1 tablespoon of oil to a large casserole dish, toss in the shallots, and stir around the dish for a few minutes until just starting to brown. Add the tomato paste, spices, and bay leaves and cook for 2 more minutes.

2 Add the tomatoes, maple syrup, vinegar, and drained beans along with 2 cups (500ml) water; season; and bring to a gentle simmer. Cook, uncovered, for 20 minutes.

3 Preheat the oven to 400°F (200°C). Line a baking sheet with parchment paper, drizzle the remaining tablespoon of olive oil over the sheet. Add the crushed garlic and mushroom ketchup, season, and add the mushrooms. Use your hands to coat the mushrooms in the mix, then spread the mushrooms out with their undersides facing up. Top with the thyme sprigs. Roast for 15–20 minutes, basting with juices halfway through.

4 When the beans are cooked, remove from the heat and stir through the roasted mushrooms together with any cooking juices. Sprinkle with parsley and serve with cornbread muffins.

HYBRID MAC 'N' CHEESE

This vegan mac 'n' cheese adds a new twist to this classic, with less cheese and more veg. A creamy sauce is made with blended butternut squash, and the dish is finished with a crispy fried onion crumb.

Serves 4

Prep 10 mins
Cook 45 mins

10oz (300g) macaroni
1lb 5oz (600g) butternut squash, peeled and cut into 2in (5cm) chunks
1 onion, chopped
3 tbsp olive oil
4 tbsp all-purpose flour
1¾ cups (400ml) soy milk
fresh nutmeg
4¼oz (120g) vegan Cheddar cheese
2 tbsp dried breadcrumbs
2 tbsp crispy fried onions
1 tsp dried sage
freshly ground black pepper

8 x 12in (20 x 30cm) baking dish

1   Bring a large pan of salted water to a boil. Add the pasta and cook for 8 minutes or until al dente, drain, and set aside.

2   Meanwhile, place the squash and onion in a large microwaveable bowl, add 2 tablespoons water, and cover with plastic wrap. Cook at full power for 8 minutes, or until tender. Leave to stand for 5 minutes.

3   Warm the olive oil over medium heat in a large pan. Stir in the flour and cook for 1 minute. Gradually add the soy milk, whisking after each addition, until incorporated. Bring to a steady simmer, constantly whisking, until the sauce has thickened. Stir in a grating of nutmeg, a good grind of black pepper, and finally the cheese.

4   Drain the cooked squash and onions. Put 16 whole chunks of the squash to one side. Add the remainder along with the onions to a blender, pour in the cheese sauce, and blend together until smooth.

5   Preheat the oven to 425°F (220°C). Add the whole chunks of squash and the pasta to the cheese sauce, stirring until everything is combined and coated. Pour into a baking dish. Combine the breadcrumbs, crispy fried onions, and sage, and scatter over the top of the dish. Bake for 30 minutes until melty, oozy, and golden on top.

LOCKED AND LOADED TORTILLA CHIPS

Loaded with refried beans, avocado, and jalapeños and served
with a spicy pineapple salsa, these tortillas chips are packed
with flavor.

Serves 4–6

Prep 15 mins
Cook 20 mins

7oz (200g) tortilla chips; we used
   blue and white corn chips
7oz (200g) refried beans
1 avocado, cut into ½in (1cm) cubes
9 mixed cherry tomatoes, quartered
12 slices of pickled jalapeño peppers
1 lime, to garnish

For the pineapple salsa
¼ small pineapple, peeled and cut
   into 4 wedges
freshly squeezed juice and zest of
   1 lime
small red chili, seeded and
   finely chopped
small handful of chopped cilantro
½ small red onion or 1 shallot,
   finely chopped

1 Preheat the oven to 275°F (140°C). Spread the tortilla chips out on
a large baking sheet and warm for 5 minutes.

2 To make the pineapple salsa, grill the pineapple on a hot ridged
stovetop grill pan for 4–5 minutes on each side, until lightly
charred. Allow to cool slightly before chopping into roughly ⅝in
(1.5cm) pieces. Squeeze over the lime juice and combine with the
chopped chili, half the cilantro, the onion, and lime zest.

3 Transfer the tortilla chips to a serving platter and spoon over the
pineapple salsa.

4 Warm the refried beans in a small pan and dot spoonfuls over the
tortilla chips. Top with the avocado, cherry tomatoes, jalapeños, and
remaining cilantro. Cut the lime into wedges to serve alongside the
dish.

BASE CAMP BAKED PASTA

This wholesome baked pasta combines meat-free "meatballs"
packed with mushrooms, bell peppers, quinoa, and sweet potato
with a rich tomato and basil sauce. Comfort food at its best.

Serves 4

Prep 20 mins
Cook 1 hour 15 mins

2 tbsp olive oil
1 red onion, finely chopped
1 red bell pepper, finely chopped
5½oz (150g) mushrooms, finely
   chopped
1 sweet potato, peeled and cut into
   large chunks
2–3 garlic cloves, crushed
¾ cup (150g) quinoa, cooked
handful of chopped flat-leaf parsley
2 tbsp sesame seeds
1 tsp smoked paprika
¼ tsp cayenne
9oz (250g) pasta of your choice;
   we used boccole
arugula, to serve
sea salt and freshly ground black
   pepper

For the tomato sauce
1 tbsp olive oil
2 fat garlic cloves, crushed
3 cups (680g) tomato paste
2 tsp balsamic vinegar
small bunch of basil, leaves picked

1 Heat 1 tablespoon of oil in a large frying pan and sauté the onion
until translucent. Add the pepper and mushrooms, season, and
cook for 2 more minutes or until tender.

2 Meanwhile, bring a pan of water to a boil, add the sweet potato
chunks and cook for 5 minutes or until tender, then drain. Place the
sweet potato chunks in a large bowl and mash with a fork. Add the
mushroom mixture, cooked quinoa, garlic, parsley, sesame seeds,
and spices, and mix to combine well.

3 Preheat the oven to 400°F (200°C). Line a large baking sheet with
parchment paper and drizzle with the remaining tablespoon of oil.

4 When the vegetable mixture is cool enough to handle, dampen your
hands and roll 2 tablespoons of the mixture together to form balls;
the mix should make about 12 balls in total.

5 Place the veggie balls on the prepared baking sheet and bake for
about 25–30 minutes, until the outside is slightly crispy.

6 While the veggie balls are baking, bring a large pan of salted water
to a boil and cook the pasta for half the recommended cooking
time. Drain and transfer to a large baking dish.

7 To make the tomato sauce, gently heat the olive oil in a pan, and fry
the garlic for 1 minute. Pour in the tomato paste, balsamic vinegar,
and half the basil leaves. Simmer for 10 minutes.

8 Pour the tomato sauce over the pasta in the baking dish, nestle in
the veggie balls, cover the dish with foil, and bake for 20 minutes,
uncovering for the last 10 minutes of cooking time. Scatter with
the remaining basil and serve with arugula.

SCRAMBLED TOFU WRAP

Perfect "to-go food" for the rank and file, these vegan breakfast wraps pack in the flavor and nutrients, with roasted tomatoes, spinach, and black beans adding extra color to a base of turmeric-scrambled tofu.

Makes 4

Prep 10 mins
Cook 20 mins

2 tbsp olive oil
10 whole cherry tomatoes
4 large tortilla wraps
12oz (350g) silken tofu
¼ tsp ground turmeric
1½oz (40g) baby spinach leaves
1 cup (200g) canned black beans,
   drained and rinsed
1 avocado, peeled and sliced
2 green onions, sliced
4 tbsp tomato chutney, to serve
   (optional)
sea salt and freshly ground black
   pepper

1 Preheat the oven to 350°F (180°C). Line a baking sheet with parchment paper, drizzle with 1 tablespoon of olive oil, and season with a pinch of salt and a grind of pepper. Add the tomatoes and roll around the sheet to coat them in the oil. Roast for 8–10 minutes, then remove from the oven and set aside. Warm the wraps in the oven for 5 minutes.

2 Heat the remaining oil in a nonstick pan, add the tofu, and break it into small pieces with the back of a wooden spoon. Sprinkle over the turmeric, season to taste, and cook for 2 minutes.

3 When ready to serve, pile a few spinach leaves over each wrap, then divide the black beans, scrambled tofu, and roasted tomatoes between each. Top with slices of avocado and green onion. Fold up, tucking the ends in, and slice in half. Serve with tomato chutney, if you'd like.

INTERSTELLAR SOUP

This spicy tomato and black bean soup balances a chili kick with toppings of creamy avocado and feta. Serve scattered with crispy tortilla strips to add some crunch.

Serves 4

Prep 10 mins
Cook 50 mins

4⅓ cups (1 liter)) vegetable stock
2 fat red chilies; 1 pierced a
    few times with a sharp knife,
    1 seeded and sliced, to serve
    (optional)
2 whole dried ancho chilies
1 garlic bulb, cut in half horizontally
    through the center
small bunch of cilantro,
    stalks and leaves separated
1 cinnamon stick
3 tbsp vegetable oil
1 large onion, chopped
1 tbsp ground cumin
1 tbsp ground cilantro
1 tbsp smoked paprika
2 x 14oz (400g) cans chopped
    tomatoes
11oz (320g) can sweetcorn, drained
7oz (200g) canned black beans,
    drained
freshly squeezed juice and zest of
    2 limes
2 corn tortilla wraps, quartered and
    cut into strips
2 avocados
3½oz (100g) feta or vegan feta

1 Pour the vegetable stock into a pan with the whole fresh and dried chilies, garlic, cilantro stalks, and cinnamon, and set over medium heat. When the liquid comes to a boil, reduce to a gentle simmer and cover with a lid. Cook for 15 minutes, then remove from the heat and leave to infuse for 20 minutes before straining into a jug or pot, discarding the aromatics.

2 Heat 1 tablespoon of oil in a pan, add the onion, and cook for 8–10 minutes until softened. Stir in the spices and tomatoes, and pour over the stock. Season well and simmer with the lid ajar for 30 minutes.

3 Add the corn, beans, and lime juice and zest to taste, and cook for 5 more minutes.

4 Heat the remaining oil in a frying pan. Add the tortilla pieces and fry until golden and crispy, then drain on paper towel. Halve and peel the avocados, and cut into small chunks.

5 Serve the soup topped with the crispy tortilla strips, cilantro leaves, and chunks of avocado and feta. Sprinkle with the chopped chili, if you want an extra hit of heat.

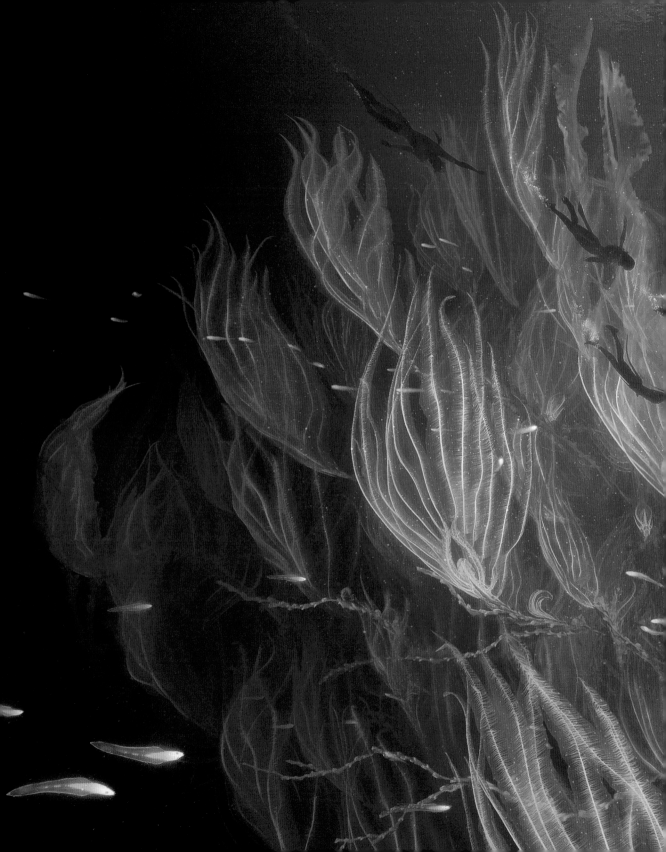

3 Metkayina Bounty

Living in harmony with the ocean, the Metkayina combine the flora and fauna of the sea in their recipes, bringing fish and seafood together in refreshing salads and finger food. Try spicy squid or a creamy chowder to connect to the ocean's spirit.

NA'VI SUPER SMOOTHIE BOWL

This vibrant smoothie gets its color from blue spirulina, an algae rich in antioxidants. With a superfood blend of banana, blueberries, and avocado, it's all you need to prepare for a day's hunting amid the ocean waves.

Serves 1

Prep 5 mins

½ banana
handful of sliced blueberries, plus
    extra to serve
¼ avocado, peeled and stoned
1 medjool date
1 cup (250ml) almond milk, or milk
    of your choice
1 tbsp blue spirulina powder

To serve
coconut flakes
hemp hearts
honey (optional)

1 Add all the ingredients to a blender, reserving a few blueberries to serve, and blend until smooth.

2 Pour the smoothie into a serving bowl and top with sliced blueberries, coconut flakes, hemp hearts, and a drizzle of honey to taste.

ZESTY SEAWALL SKEWERS

Fishing in the lagoon protected by the seawall provides the Metkayina clan with the bounty of the ocean, ready to be cooked over open fires. These simple grilled skewers of jumbo shrimp marinated in lime, lemon, and garlic are the ideal communal meal.

Makes 12

Prep 5 mins plus marinating
Cook 15 mins

freshly squeezed juice and zest of 1 lime, a little zest reserved to garnish
2 lemons
1 garlic clove, crushed
1 tbsp dark rum (optional)
12 shell-on jumbo shrimp
pinch of saffron
4 tbsp mayonnaise
2 tsp olive oil
handful of garden cress
sea salt and freshly ground black pepper

12 wooden skewers soaked in water for 30 mins

1 In a shallow bowl, combine the juice and zest of the lime and one lemon with the garlic and rum, if using. Reserve a little of the lime and lemon zest to garnish. Add the shrimp to the bowl, season, and leave to marinate in the fridge for up to 1 hour.

2 Mix the saffron into the mayonnaise, halve the remaining lemon, and add a squeeze of juice to the mayonnaise to taste. Set aside.

3 Thread each shrimp lengthwise down a skewer. Heat a grill or ridged cast-iron grill pan until smoking hot. Brush each skewer with a little olive oil and grill for 3–4 minutes on each side. Add the lemon halves and grill until lightly charred and cooked through.

4 Serve on a platter sprinkled with cress and the reserved citrus zest, with the grilled lemon to squeeze over and mayonnaise dip on the side.

CATCH-OF-THE-DAY GIANT COUSCOUS

Whether caught with a spear in the shallows or fresh from the market, a whole fish makes an impressive family meal. Here, red snapper is prepared with a herb rub and roasted with fennel, garlic, and lemon, served on a bed of giant couscous.

Serves 4

Prep 15 mins
Cook 30 mins

small handful of flat-leaf parsley
2 shallots, sliced
1 garlic clove, roughly chopped
4 sprigs of thyme, leaves picked
2 lemons
2 tbsp olive oil
1 large fennel bulb, sliced
2¼lbs (1kg) whole red snapper, gutted and scaled
1⅓ cups (200g) pearl couscous
sea salt and freshly ground black pepper

1 Preheat the oven to 400°F (200°C).

2 Add the parsley, shallots, garlic, thyme, and zest of 1 lemon to a food processor and process until finely chopped. Pour in the oil and process until well incorporated, about 15 seconds. Spoon half this mix onto a large, shallow baking sheet. Add the fennel and toss together to coat; season well.

3 Cut three 2in (5cm)-long diagonal slits on both sides of fish, all the way to the bone. Rub the remaining herb mixture into the outside and inside of the cuts. Nestle the fish in the center of the baking sheet. Slice the remaining lemon and arrange the slices around the edge. Bake in the preheated oven until the fish is opaque and flaky and the fennel is tender, about 30 minutes.

4 While the fish is cooking, boil the couscous following the package instructions.

5 When the fish is cooked, spoon the couscous around the edges of the fish in the baking sheet and stir to combine with the fennel and cooking juices. Serve at the table with a green salad.

REEF BITES

Transport yourself to the underwater reef with these juicy bites that combine crab meat with cilantro and lime in pan-fried crispy patties.

Makes 12 as an appetizer or canapé

Prep 10 mins plus chilling
Cook 20 mins

7oz (200g) white crab meat
1 tbsp mayonnaise
1 tbsp red Thai curry paste
4 tbsp panko breadcrumbs
1 lime
handful of chopped cilantro
2 green onions, finely sliced
1 egg, lightly beaten
3 tbsp dried coconut
sunflower oil
handful of chives, roughly snipped, to garnish

For the dip
4 tbsp mayonnaise
2 tbsp caviar (optional)
pinch of snipped chives

1 In a bowl, add the crab meat, mayonnaise, curry paste, 2 tablespoons of breadcrumbs, juice and zest of ½ the lime, chopped cilantro, and green onions and gently stir together. Pour in enough egg to bind together to make a sticky mix. Take about 1 tablespoon at a time and shape into 12 neat, round patties. Transfer these to a plate and put in the refrigerator for 20 minutes to firm up.

2 For the dip, mix the mayonnaise with the chives and caviar and spoon into a serving dish.

3 Combine the coconut and remaining breadcrumbs in a small bowl. Gently press each patty into the breadcrumb mix, slightly flattening it with your hand, and coat both sides.

4 Preheat the oven to 275°F (140°C). Add enough sunflower oil to a shallow frying pan to come about ½in (1cm) up the side. Heat the oil, then carefully add the crab cakes 4 at a time. Cook for about 3 minutes on each side until they are crisp and golden. Drain on paper towel. At this point, you can put the crab cakes into the low-heat oven to keep warm while you cook the remaining patties.

5 Slice the remaining lime half into wedges and serve with the crab cakes and dip, sprinkled with chives. Add the caviar if desired.

SPICY SQUID MORSELS

A Pandoran variation of salt and pepper squid, these crispy morsels are glazed with red pepper jelly to give them an extra flavor hit.

Serves 4

Prep 15 mins
Cook 20 mins

1 tsp white peppercorns
1 tsp Sichuan peppercorns
1 tsp sea salt
½ cup (60g) all-purpose flour
¼ cup (40g) rice flour
16 prepared baby squid
vegetable oil, for deep-frying
4 garlic cloves, sliced
1 red chili, seeded and
    sliced
2 tbsp red pepper jelly
1 tbsp rice wine vinegar

To garnish
handful of Thai basil leaves
2 green onions, finely
    sliced

1 Dry roast the peppercorns in a wok or frying pan over medium–high heat for 3–4 minutes or until fragrant. Use a pestle and mortar or food processor to grind the peppercorns with the salt to a fine powder. Combine with the flours and transfer to a baking sheet.

2 Clean and pat the squid pieces with paper towel to remove excess moisture and lightly score the flat pieces on the inside with a table knife. Coat all the squid pieces in the flour mix.

3 Heat the oil in a deep-sided pan to 338ºF /170ºC. If you don't have a thermometer, you can test the temperature with a cube of bread —it should brown in 20 seconds.

4 When the oil is at temperature, fry the squid in batches for 2–3 minutes or until light golden in color. Drain on paper towel.

5 Heat a tablespoon of vegetable oil in the wok. Stir-fry the garlic and chilli until just turning golden, around 30 seconds. Add the red pepper jelly and squid to the wok, drizzle over the rice wine vinegar, and stir-fry quickly in the aromatic mixture for about a minute. Serve immediately, garnished with basil leaves and green onions.

CLAN CHOWDER

This creamy broth combines flaked hot-smoked salmon with chunks of potato and corn, with a hit of heat from jalapeño chilies. Nourishing and warming, it embodies Tonowari's care of his clan.

Serves 4

Prep 15 mins
Cook 45 mins

2 tbsp unsalted butter
4 rashers smoked bacon,
   cut into 1in (3cm) pieces
3 celery sticks, sliced
4 shallots, peeled and thinly sliced
1 jalapeño pepper, seeded and
   thinly sliced
1 tsp smoked paprika
4 garlic cloves, minced
6¼ cups (1.5 liters) chicken stock
8 new potatoes, unpeeled, cut into
   ¾in (2cm) dice
1½ tsp sea salt
½ tsp freshly ground black pepper
1 tbsp cornstarch
1 cup (200g) frozen corn
1 cup (200ml) heavy cream
2 hot-smoked salmon fillets (about
   5½oz/160g)
a few snipped chives, to garnish
crusty bread, to serve

1 Melt the butter in a frying pan and sauté the bacon until crisp. Set aside (leaving the fat in the pan). Add the celery, shallots, jalapeños, smoked paprika, and garlic to the frying pan and cook until everything has softened, about 5–6 minutes.

2 In a large pan, bring the chicken stock to a simmer, add the potatoes, and cook until tender, about 10 minutes.

3 Add the bacon and the softened vegetables to the stock, and return to a gentle simmer.

4 Whisk the cornstarch into a little water, then stir the starchy paste into the chowder base, bring to a gentle rolling boil, and cook for 10 minutes. Reduce the heat and stir in the corn and cream. Heat through gently until the corn is cooked.

5 Remove from the heat and flake the salmon pieces on top of the chowder. Cover with a lid and allow to sit for 10 minutes or until the salmon is warmed through. Spoon between bowls and garnish with snipped chives. Serve warm with crusty bread.

SEA SHIMMER POKE BOWL

Reflecting all the rich colors of the bioluminescent coral reef, this bright poke bowl brings together raw salmon with sushi rice, avocado, edamame, radish, mango, and cucumber, served with a zingy teriyaki sauce.

Serves 4

Prep 15 mins
Cook 30 mins

¼ small red cabbage, cut into 2
    wedges
1 cup (190g) uncooked brown sushi
    rice
1 tbsp sushi vinegar
1lb (480g) very fresh (sushi-grade)
    skinless salmon fillet, cut into ½in
    (1cm) cubes
2 tsp ponzu sauce
1 tsp sesame oil
½ small red chili, seeded
    and chopped
⅔ cup (100g) edamame beans
8 radishes, sliced
¼ cucumber, diced
½ small mango, diced
2 tbsp teriyaki sauce
sesame seeds, to garnish

1 Bring the required amount of water for the sushi rice to a boil, add half the cabbage and the rice to the pan, and cook following the packet instructions. Allow to cool completely, then discard the cabbage and stir through the sushi vinegar.

2 Marinate the salmon in the ponzu sauce for 10 minutes.

3 Thinly slice the remaining raw cabbage and dress with sesame oil and chilli.

4 Assemble the bowls. Start by dividing the cooled rice between the bowls, then top with a portion each of salmon, edamame, radish, cucumber, mango, and dressed cabbage. Drizzle over the teriyaki sauce and garnish with a sprinkle of sesame seeds.

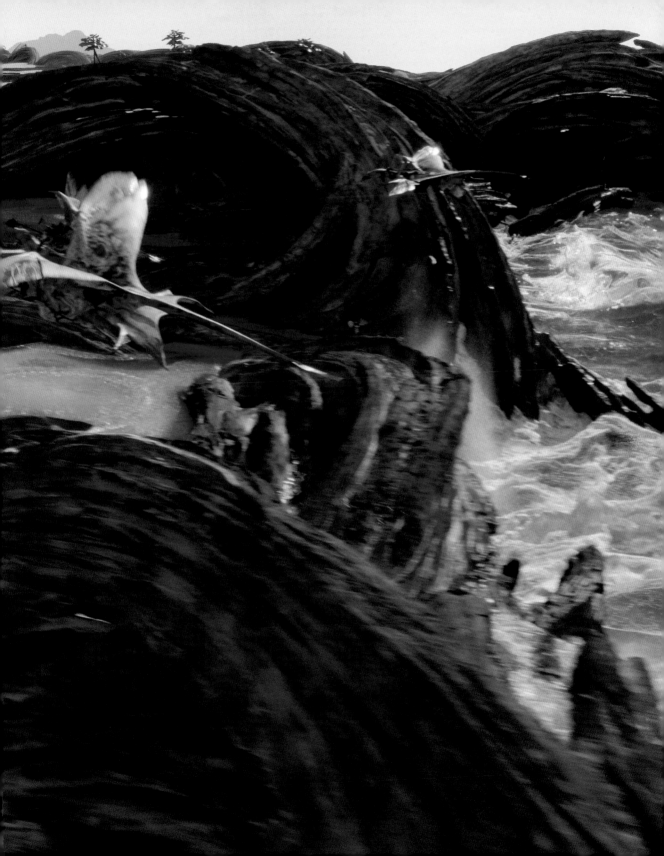

OCEAN ORZO

Orzo pasta has a delicious chewy texture and makes the
perfect base to absorb the flavors of garlic and herbs from
the mussel broth.

Serves 4

Prep 5 mins
Cook 20 mins

7oz (200g) orzo
1 tbsp olive oil, plus extra to serve
4 shallots, sliced into rounds
16 cherry tomatoes, halved
1 tbsp tomato paste
pinch of saffron
2 garlic cloves, thinly sliced
1 bay leaf
4 cups (900ml) chicken stock
2¼lb (1kg) prepared mussels
1 lemon
small handful of chopped flat-leaf
    parsley

1 Put the orzo into a medium-sized bowl, cover with boiling water,
and set aside to soak for 15 minutes, then drain and rinse.

2 Heat the oil in a large, lidded sauté pan over medium–low heat;
add the shallots; and fry gently for about 8 minutes, or until
softened but not colored.

3 Add the tomatoes, tomato paste, saffron, garlic, and bay leaf.
Stir-fry for 2 minutes, then pour over the stock and simmer for
3 minutes.

4 Add the orzo, then spread the mussels on top. Cover with a lid,
reduce the heat, and cook for 5 minutes, or until the mussels have
all opened. Discard any mussels that remain closed.

5 Squeeze plenty of lemon juice over the mussels, sprinkle with
parsley, and drizzle with olive oil to serve.

ATOLL TUNA SALAD

For this hearty salad, slices of sesame-crusted, pan-seared tuna are served on a bed of sprouted alfalfa, mango, and cucumber, topped with a punchy dressing.

Serves 4

Prep 15 mins plus marinating
Cook 5 mins

1 tbsp soy sauce
2in (5cm) piece of fresh root ginger, peeled and grated
1 garlic clove, grated
4 tuna steaks, about 14oz (400g) total weight
2 tbsp black and white sesame seeds
1 red chili, seeded and finely chopped
1 tbsp crispy fried onions

For the cilantro dressing
2in (5cm) piece of fresh ginger root, peeled and thinly sliced
1 garlic clove
1 red chili, seeded and thinly sliced
small handful of cilantro
½ ripe mango, diced
3 tbsp olive oil
3 tbsp rice wine vinegar

For the salad
1½ ripe mangoes, thinly sliced
3oz (80g) snow peas, shredded
½ cucumber, shaved into ribbons
large handful of alfalfa or pea shoots

1 Mix the soy sauce with the grated ginger and garlic in a shallow dish. Add the tuna steaks and coat with this mix. Set aside to marinate for 30 minutes.

2 Make the cilantro dressing: add all the ingredients to a blender and process into a smooth sauce. Set aside until ready to serve.

3 Arrange the salad ingredients on a serving platter or board.

4 Spread half the sesame seeds over a plate and lay the tuna steaks on top. Sprinkle the remaining sesame seeds over the top of the steaks to coat.

5 Warm a nonstick pan over medium–high heat, add the olive oil, and sear the tuna, about 30 seconds to 1 minute on each side, depending on how well-cooked you like it. Cut the tuna into ½in (1cm)-thick slices and arrange over the salad. Spoon over the dressing and sprinkle the chili and crispy fried onions on top.

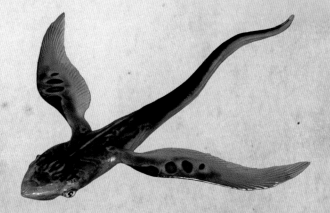

ZINGY FLASH-FRIED SHRIMP

Perfect finger food for sharing, these pan-fried shrimp are coated in a garlicky crumb served with salty samphire. Roast lemon adds a sweetness that brings everything together in harmony.

Serves 2

Prep 15 mins
Cook 30 mins

2 lemons, cut into ¼in (5mm) slices
3 garlic cloves, unpeeled
2 tbsp olive oil
2 thick slices of sourdough bread
small handful of flat-leaf parsley
24 jumbo shrimp
6oz (180g) samphire or asparagus

1 Preheat the oven to 350ºF (180ºC). Lay the lemon slices on a lined baking sheet, add 2 whole unpeeled garlic cloves, drizzle with a teaspoon of olive oil, and roast for 20 minutes.

2 Tear the bread into the bowl of a food processor and process to a rough crumb. Peel and roughly chop the remaining garlic and add to the breadcrumbs along with the parsley and 2 teaspoons of olive oil. Pulse to combine.

3 Add the garlic breadcrumbs to a dry frying pan and toast over a low heat until crisp and golden. Set aside and wipe the pan.

4 Set the pan back over high heat, drizzle in the remaining olive oil, toss in the shrimp, and season. Fry for 4–5 minutes, then add the samphire and roasted lemon slices and any cooking juices. Squeeze the roasted garlic from the skins into the pan and cook for another minute.

5 Transfer the contents of the pan to a serving platter and top with the toasted breadcrumbs to serve.

DIVER'S BOUNTY PASTA

Full of the flavors of the sea, squid ink linguine provides a base
for a seafood mix of mussels, shrimp, and squid, balanced with
fresh bursts of capers, garlic, and cherry tomatoes.

Serves 4

Prep 5 mins
Cook 15 mins

14oz (400g) squid ink linguine
2 tbsp olive oil
2 shallots, finely chopped
2 garlic cloves, thinly sliced
2 tbsp capers
7oz (200g) seafood mix (store-
    bought or a personalized
    combination of mussels, squid,
    and shrimp)
1 tbsp tomato paste
6oz (180g) cherry tomatoes, halved
freshly squeezed juice of 1 lemon
small handful of chopped flat-leaf
    parsley, to serve

1   Bring a large pan of salted water to a boil and cook the pasta until
    al dente, following the package instructions.

2   While the pasta is cooking, add 1 tablespoon of olive oil to a pan
    and fry the shallots until softened, then add the garlic and capers
    and cook for another minute.

3   Add a splash more oil to the pan and toss in the seafood, tomato
    paste, cherry tomatoes, half the lemon juice, and a couple of
    tablespoons of pasta cooking water. Cook for 1–2 minutes, or until
    the seafood is fully heated through and all the mussels have
    opened. Discard any mussels that remain closed. If you need to
    wait for the pasta to cook, remove the seafood from the heat.

4   When the pasta is ready, use tongs to transfer the cooked pasta
    directly into the pan and toss together to coat everything in the
    sauce. Squeeze over the remaining lemon juice and sprinkle with
    the parsley to serve.

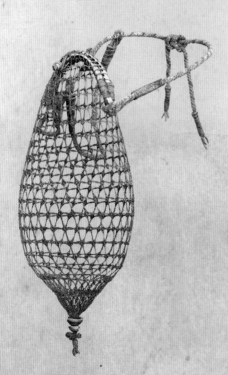

SHORELINE SALAD

The bounty of the sea extends to flora, too, and here wakame seaweed is combined with refreshing cucumber and toasted sesame seeds in a harmonious salad to serve alongside a seafood feast.

Serves 4 as a side

Prep 10 mins

1oz (30g) wakame
2 tbsp sesame oil
3 tbsp rice wine vinegar
pinch of sea salt
1 large cucumber
1 tbsp toasted sesame seeds
1 tsp crushed red pepper flakes, optional

1 Rehydrate the wakame in enough warm water to cover it while you prepare the other ingredients.

2 Whisk together the oil, vinegar, and salt in a large bowl. Slice the cucumber in half lengthwise; scoop out the seeds and discard. Cut the cucumber into 5mm (¼in) slices and add to the dressing.

3 Drain the wakame and pat dry with paper towel, then toss through the cucumber salad and transfer to a serving bowl. Top with toasted sesame seeds and chili flakes.

SEAGRASS TOFU STACKS

Packed with umami flavors of red cabbage and pink pickled ginger, these sushi-inspired tofu stacks are wrapped in sheets of nori seaweed. They make the perfect snack after exploring the reef and training with the ilu.

Serves 4

Prep 10 mins
Cook 10 mins plus 20 mins to assemble

1 tbsp soy sauce, plus extra for dipping
1 tsp curry powder
7oz (200g) firm tofu
1 tbsp sunflower oil
4 tbsp cornstarch
6 sheets sushi nori seaweed
1 cup (190g) sushi rice, cooked to package instructions
large handful of baby spinach
4 radishes, thinly sliced
1 avocado, peeled and sliced
¾oz (20g) pickled ginger, plus extra to serve

1 Combine the soy sauce and curry powder. Cut the tofu into 6 blocks roughly ½in (1cm) thick and 3½in (9cm) square. Spread the tofu on a baking tray and pour over the soy mix.

2 Heat the oil in a nonstick frying pan over medium heat. Dip each tofu slice into the cornstarch, and fry two at a time for 3–4 minutes on each side until crisp. Drain on kitchen paper to get rid of excess oil.

3 To assemble, cut a square of plastic wrap a little larger than the nori sheet, and place a nori sheet on top shiny-side down, with a point of the sheet facing toward you. Wet your hands and take a handful of rice, place it in the middle of the sheet, and shape into a rough 3½in (9cm) square.

4 Stack layers of spinach, radish, avocado, and a slice of tofu on top and finish with pickled ginger.

5 Overlap all four corners of the nori sheet on top of the filling, using a little water to seal. Finally, gather all the plastic wrap over the stack and tie on the top. Repeat to make 4 stacks. Set aside to let the seaweed soften a little.

6 When ready to serve, remove the plastic wrap and cut the stack in half with a sharp knife. Serve with soy sauce on the side and extra pickled ginger.

SMOKED TROUT ROLLS

With a balance of fresh and zesty flavors, these bite-sized rolls make the ideal offering for shared meals. Pair with Seagrass Tofu Stacks on page 118 for a finger-food feast.

Makes 12

Prep 10 mins

1 cucumber
½ cup (100g) cream cheese
1 tsp horseradish
1 tbsp chopped dill, plus extra to garnish
2 tsp capers, roughly chopped
freshly squeezed juice and zest of ½ lemon
4¼oz (120g) smoked trout

1 Use a wide vegetable peeler to shave 12 long strips from the length of the cucumber. Lay out on paper towel to remove any excess water.

2 In a bowl, combine the cream cheese, horseradish, dill, capers, and lemon juice and zest.

3 Lay a strip of smoked trout on one end of each piece of cucumber and spread a heaped teaspoon of cream cheese mixture halfway along the length of the cucumber strip. Roll into a spiral and place on a serving plate, garnished with a scattering of dill fronds.

Clan Feasts

4

The Na'vi often come together to reaffirm their connections to each other and with Eywa. These recipes are perfect if you're planning a gathering, with celebration cakes and sharing platters that would make a fine spread under any canopy.

PANDORAN PARTY PLATTER

This rainbow-hued platter makes a great party centerpiece,
bringing together a tropical selection of fruits with lime and mango
cheesecake- and chocolate-flavored dips.

Serves 6–8

Prep 30 mins

tropical fruit of choice, such as
mango, dragon fruit, pineapple,
melon, plums, kiwi, strawberry,
and pomegranate seeds, enough
for your party size
3½oz (100g) pretzels
4 graham crackers (2oz/60g)
processed to a crumb

For the cheesecake dip
½ cup (100g) mascarpone
1 tsp vanilla extract
2 tbsp powdered sugar
freshly squeezed juice and zest of
½ lime
3½oz (100g) mango

For the chocolate dip
5½oz (150g) dark chocolate
½ cup (200ml) coconut cream
2 tbsp superfine sugar

1 Prepare the fruit as necessary, slicing and dicing to provide
bite-sized pieces, using star-shaped cookie cutters to slice any
leftovers as decoration. Arrange the fruit in a pleasing display on
a large platter.

2 Fill a serving bowl with pretzels and another with the graham
cracker crumbs.

3 For the cheesecake dip, add the mascarpone, vanilla, powdered
sugar, lime juice, and mango to a blender and process until smooth
and fluffy. Spoon into a serving bowl, and top with the lime zest.

4 For the chocolate dip, melt all the ingredients with 2 tablespoons
cold water in short bursts in a microwave, or in a heat-resistant
bowl over a pan of lightly simmering water, taking care not to let
the chocolate get too hot. Allow to cool slightly before pouring into
a serving bowl. Arrange all the bowls around the platter for dipping
and snacking.

Tip
For a vegan option, replace the mascarpone with 3½oz (100g) of
soaked cashews.

BLUE SEAS TEAR-AND-SHARE GARLIC BREAD

The pretty butterfly pea flower is the secret ingredient that gives this garlic bread its natural blue color, in honor of the Pandoran oceans. Serve at a celebration to share in true Na'vi style.

Makes 16

Prep 30 mins
Cook 1 hour 15 mins plus proofing

1¼ cups (275ml) whole milk
1 tbsp butterfly pea flower tea (blue tea), or a couple of drops of blue food coloring
3¾ cups (450g) strong white bread flour
2¼ tsp (7g) dried active yeast
½ tsp fine salt
1 tsp superfine sugar
1 garlic bulb
1 tsp olive oil, plus extra for greasing
7 tbsp (100g) salted butter, softened
small handful of chopped flat-leaf parsley
2 sprigs of rosemary, leaves picked
1 egg, lightly beaten

9in (23cm) springform cake pan

1 Gently warm the milk until it just starts to steam. Remove from the heat and add the butterfly pea flowers. Set aside to infuse for 20 minutes, then strain the blue milk into a pitcher, discarding the butterfly pea flowers.

2 Add the flour, yeast, salt, and sugar to the bowl of a stand mixer with a dough hook attachment. With the mixer running on low speed, pour in the milk, increase the speed to medium, and run for 10 minutes to form a sticky dough.

3 Oil a clean bowl and use an oiled spatula to transfer the dough. Cover with plastic wrap and leave to rise at room temperature for 1 hour, or until doubled in size.

4 Preheat the oven to 400°F (200°C). Slice the top third off the garlic bulb, drizzle with olive oil, and wrap in foil. Roast in the oven for 30–35 minutes.

5 When cool enough to handle, squeeze the roasted garlic into a bowl and mash with a fork into a paste. Add the softened butter and chopped parsley and set aside at room temperature.

6 Line the base of a springform cake pan with parchment paper. Rub 1 tablespoon of the garlic butter around the edges.

7 Lightly dust the work surface with flour, turn the dough out, and sprinkle over the rosemary. Knead lightly for 1 minute.

8 Weigh the dough and divide into 16 equal portions, shaping each into a neat ball where the dough is smooth and stretched underneath with a seam on top.

9 With the seams on the underside, arrange the dough balls in the springform tin, starting around the outer edge with 10 balls, leaving a little gap between each one to allow for rising. Continue with 5 balls inside the outer ring, and finish with the last dough ball in the center.

10 Cover loosely with lightly oiled plastic wrap and leave to rise at room temperature for 45 more minutes, or until doubled in size.

11 Preheat the oven to 400°F (200°C). Brush the dough balls with the beaten egg and dot the garlic butter over the top. Bake on the middle shelf of the oven for 25–30 minutes, or until risen and golden brown. Release from the pan and serve right away.

SANCTUARY STEW

This stew of slow-braised pork shoulder with chunks of pumpkin or squash is a hearty family meal that rewards the long cooking time with tender meat in a rich and satisfying sauce.

Serves 6

Prep 10 mins
Cook 2 hours 45 mins

2 tbsp cumin seeds
2 tbsp fennel seeds
1 tbsp all-purpose flour
1lb 5oz (600g) pork shoulder cut
    into 4in (10cm) pieces
2 tbsp sunflower oil
12 shallots, peeled and halved
4 garlic cloves, crushed
2 tbsp tomato paste
2 tbsp Dijon mustard
12fl oz (330ml) pale ale
4¼ cups (1 liter) chicken stock
1 tbsp red wine vinegar
2 strips of orange zest
2 bay leaves
1lb 5oz (600g) pumpkin or squash,
    peeled and cut into 2in (5cm)
    chunks
sea salt

To serve
3½oz (100g) kale, shredded
Blue Seas Tear-and-Share Garlic
    Bread, see page 128

1 Toast the cumin and fennel seeds in a dry pan over low heat until fragrant. Grind with 1 teaspoon of salt in a food processor or a pestle and mortar to a fine powder and combine with the flour.

2 Sprinkle the flour and spice mix over the pork and toss to coat. Heat 1 tablespoon of oil in a large, lidded casserole, and brown the meat in batches.

3 Add all the browned meat back to the pan along with the shallots, garlic, tomato paste, and mustard. Cook over low heat for a couple of minutes before pouring in the ale, stock, and vinegar. Bring to a low simmer, add the orange zest and bay leaves, and cook, covered, for 2 hours.

4 Use a slotted spoon to lift the pork onto a plate and loosely cover with foil. Leave the meat to rest while the pumpkin cooks.

5 Place the pumpkin chunks in the sauce, replace the lid, and cook for 30 more minutes. When the pumpkin is tender, shred the pork using two forks and add back to the pan to heat through.

6 Cook the kale in salted, boiling water until just tender, and serve alongside the stew with tear-and-share garlic bread.

HOMETREE PLATTER

For the perfect Hometree gathering, serve up avocado and cilantro dip paired with spiced turmeric hummus, smothered over a board with crudités and crackers.

Serves 8–10

Prep 20 mins

For the hummus
14oz (2 x 400g) cans chickpeas, drained and rinsed
6 tbsp tahini
6 tbsp extra virgin olive oil, plus extra to serve
2 garlic cloves, crushed
½ tsp ground cumin
freshly squeezed lemon juice, to taste
1 tsp grated fresh turmeric
2 avocados, peeled and pitted
small handful of chopped cilantro leaves, plus extra to serve
sea salt and freshly ground black pepper

For the crudités
4 rainbow carrots, peeled and sliced into batons
2 heads of endive, leaves separated
5½oz (150g) mixed radishes
selection of breadsticks and crackers

To serve
pinch of za'atar spice mix
3oz (80g) mixed olives, sliced

1 To make the hummus, put the chickpeas into the bowl of a food processor along with ½ cup (120ml) cold water, and blend together until smooth.

2 Add the tahini, olive oil, garlic, cumin, and lemon juice, and blend again briefly to combine. Season to taste.

3 Spoon out half the hummus into a bowl, mix through the grated turmeric, and spread onto a large serving board. Smooth with the back of a spoon to cover one half of the board.

4 Add the avocados and chopped cilantro to the blender with the remaining hummus and blend again until smooth. Spread the avocado hummus over the other half of the serving board, and top with a few cilantro leaves.

5 Build the crudités and crackers around the hummus in a rainbow of color. Scatter with sliced olives and a pinch of za'atar, and drizzle with olive oil, ready to serve.

LUMINESCENT ICE POPS

Capturing the swirling luminescent clouds and spectacular
sunsets of Pandora, these multisensory ice pops combine
bubble tea pearls with fruit juices in colorful layers.

Makes 6

Prep 5 mins
Freezing 3 hours

6 heaped tsp passion fruit boba
  (bubble tea pearls)
1 cup (260ml) limeade or 2 tbsp lime
  cordial mixed with ¾ cup (180ml)
  water
1 tbsp prickly pear syrup, or a red
  berry cordial, such as raspberry
2 tbsp green apple syrup
½ cup (120ml) apple juice

6 whole ice pop molds
6 wooden ice pop sticks

1 Add 1 heaped teaspoon of passion fruit boba pearls to the bottom
of each ice pop mold. Pour the limeade into a pitcher and stir in the
prickly pear syrup. Pour about 1 tablespoon of this mix into each of
the molds; set the rest aside for later. Freeze the molds until just
set, about 1 hour.

2 When the first layer is fully set remove from the freezer, combine
the green apple syrup and apple juice and top up the molds. Insert
a stick into each and return to the freezer to set.

3 When set, top up each mold with the remaining pink mix from step
1, and return to the freezer.

4 When ready to eat, allow the ice pop mold to stand at room
temperature for 5 minutes before carefully removing each ice pop.

TOTEM DIP

This vibrant dip of beets, feta, and walnut makes an ideal snack on its own, or mix and match with the Hometree Platter on page 134 and serve with homemade flatbreads on the side.

Serves 4 as an appetizer

Prep 15 mins
Cook 1 hour

10oz (300g) beets, peeled
   and cut into quarters
4 garlic cloves, unpeeled
2 tbsp olive oil
1 tsp ground cumin
1½oz (40g) walnut halves
1¾oz (50g) feta cheese
3 tbsp Greek-style yogurt
small handful of chopped flat-leaf
   parsley
sea salt

For the flatbreads
1 cup (140g) self-rising flour
½ cup (140g) Greek-style yogurt
1 tbsp olive oil

1. Preheat the oven to 400°F (200°C). Place the beets and garlic in a baking dish and drizzle with 1 tablespoon of olive oil. Add the cumin and salt, then cover the dish with foil. Roast for about 45 minutes, until the beets are tender. Leave to cool.

2. Spread the walnuts over a baking sheet and toast in the oven for the last 5 minutes of cooking time.

3. To make the flatbreads, mix the flour, yogurt, and ¼ teaspoon of salt with the oil into a rough dough. Turn out onto your work surface and knead until smooth. Divide the dough into 4 equal balls, dust with a little flour, and roll out into rough circles about ⅛in (3mm) thick.

4. Heat a heavy-bottomed pan to medium-hot and cook the flatbreads for 2–3 minutes on each side, until toasted and puffed up.

5. Transfer the cooled beets and walnuts into a food processor along with the feta, remaining tablespoon of olive oil, and yogurt. Keep a few walnuts and a little feta for garnish. Squeeze in the roasted garlic from their skins and blend until smooth. Season to taste, and stir through the parsley, keeping a little to garnish. Add a splash of water if you feel the dip is too thick.

6. Spoon the beets and feta dip into a serving bowl, and top with a drizzle of olive oil and the remaining parsley. Chop the reserved walnuts and sprinkle over the dip along with a little crumbled feta. Serve with the warm flatbreads.

HALLELUJAH CELEBRATION CAKE

This marbled vanilla and blueberry bundt cake captures the magnetic vortex that keeps the Hallelujah Mountains floating in midair. With a zingy lemon and blueberry glaze, it's the perfect way to celebrate at a Pandora-themed party.

Serves 12–16

Prep 15 mins
Cook 1 hour plus cooling

oil, for greasing
1 cup (210ml) sour cream
¼ tsp baking soda
1½ sticks (180g) unsalted butter, at
    room temperature
1½ cups (300g) superfine sugar
1 tsp vanilla extract
3 extra-large eggs, lightly beaten
zest of ½ lemon
3 cups (375g) all-purpose flour,
    plus extra for dusting
1½ tsp baking powder
1¾ cups (180g) powdered sugar
8 edible flowers, to decorate

For the blueberry sauce
1¼ cups (250g) fresh blueberries,
    plus a few extra to decorate
freshly squeezed juice of ½ lemon
1 tbsp superfine sugar

1lb (500g) bundt pan

1 To make the blueberry sauce, put the blueberries, lemon juice, sugar, and 2 tablespoons water in a pan and cook over medium heat, mashing down the berries with a fork until the sauce has thickened slightly, about 10 minutes. Push the sauce through a fine sieve to remove the berry seeds and skins. Divide the sauce between two bowls and set aside to cool.

2 Preheat the oven to 350ºF (180ºC). Lightly grease a bundt pan with a little oil and coat with flour, tapping out any excess.

3 Combine the sour cream and baking soda and set aside. In a large bowl, cream together the butter, sugar, and vanilla until pale and fluffy. Add the eggs a splash at a time, mixing to fully incorporate after each addition, then add the sour cream mixture, and half the lemon zest. Beat again briefly so that everything is well combined.

4 Sift over the flour and baking powder, and gently fold everything together into a smooth batter. Dot teaspoonfuls of one half of the blueberry sauce over the batter, and gently swirl it through to create a marbled effect. Carefully spoon into the prepared tin and bake for 40–45 minutes, or until a toothpick inserted into the center of the cake comes out clean. Set on a wire rack and leave to cool in the pan for 30 minutes.

5 While the cake is cooling, make the glaze. Sift the powdered sugar into a bowl and pour over the remaining blueberry sauce. Whisk until smooth and the texture of light cream, adding a little water or lemon juice if too thick.

6 Turn the cake out onto a wire rack and allow to cool completely. When ready to decorate, set a plate underneath the cake to catch any excess glaze. Spoon over the glaze and, when set, carefully transfer the cake to a serving plate and decorate with a few sliced blueberries, edible flowers, and the remaining lemon zest.

CHOCOLATE BARK OFFERING

Topped with pistachios, goji berries, pumpkin seeds, and bee pollen, this superfood chocolate bark is an indulgent and joyful offering from Eywa.

Serves 6–8 as a snack

Prep 10 mins
Cook 10 mins plus setting

7oz (200g) dark chocolate, chopped
1 tbsp goji berries
1 tbsp pumpkin seeds
1 tsp bee pollen
small handful of unsalted pistachios
1¾oz (50g) white chocolate, chopped
1 tsp dried raspberry powder
1 tsp matcha powder

1 Line a baking sheet with parchment paper. Melt the dark chocolate either in a heat-resistant bowl set over a pan of gently simmering water or in short bursts in the microwave, taking care not to let the chocolate get too hot.

2 Pour the dark chocolate onto the prepared baking sheet and use the back of a spoon to spread it out into a rough rectangle. Scatter over the goji berries, pumpkin seeds, bee pollen, and pistachios.

3 Melt the white chocolate in the same way as the dark chocolate, stir in the raspberry powder until blended, and use a teaspoon to drizzle the white chocolate over the top of the dark chocolate. Sprinkle the matcha powder on top.

4 Leave the chocolate bark to set for 30 minutes at room temperature, or 10 minutes in the refrigerator. Use a sharp knife to break the slab into rough pieces. Store in an airtight container for up to a week.

CELEBRATORY CLAN ROAST

This lamb dish, slow-roasted over layers of potatoes, would be perfect for a special occasion like the completion of a warrior's Iknimaya, where everyone comes together to help prepare and enjoy a celebratory meal.

Serves 6–8

Prep 15 mins
Cook 2 hours 45 mins plus resting

2 tbsp (30g) salted butter
3lb 3oz (1.5kg) potatoes, unpeeled, sliced into ⅛in (2mm) slices
2 large onions, cut into thin rounds
1¾ cups (400ml) chicken stock
5lb (2.25kg) leg of lamb
2 large sprigs of rosemary, leaves picked and finely chopped
small bunch of flat-leaf parsley
6 anchovy fillets
2 fat garlic cloves, roughly chopped
freshly squeezed juice and zest of 1 lemon
1 tbsp olive oil
sea salt and freshly ground black pepper
buttered greens, to serve

1 Preheat the oven to 350°F (180°C). Smear the butter over the sides of a large roasting pan and season with salt and pepper. Lay the potatoes and onions in an even layer over the base of the pan, pour the stock over the potatoes, and cover tightly with foil.

2 Make three slashes in the top of the lamb joint and place it in a second roasting pan.

3 Pile the herbs, anchovies, garlic, and lemon zest on your chopping board and roughly chop together to a fine mix. Combine with the oil and smooth over the surface of the lamb joint, working the rub into the cuts. Cover with foil, add to the oven with the potato pan and roast for 2 hours.

4 Remove both pans from the oven, uncover the potatoes, and carefully transfer the lamb joint on top of the potatoes. Squeeze over the lemon juice and return to the oven to roast for 45 more minutes.

5 Allow to rest for 20 minutes lightly covered with foil. Serve with buttered greens.

SWEET AND STICKY CHICKEN

Pineapple adds a refreshing sweetness to the marinade for these sticky baked chicken thighs, served with extra roasted pineapple chunks, red bell pepper, and wild rice.

Serves 4

Prep 10 mins plus marinating
Cook 45 mins

½ pineapple, peeled and cut into
   2in (5cm) chunks
1 tbsp soy sauce
2in (5cm) piece of fresh root ginger,
   peeled and grated
2 garlic cloves, crushed
freshly squeezed juice and zest of
   1 lime
pinch of ground allspice
8 skin-on, bone-in chicken thighs
1 red bell pepper
2 sprigs of thyme
1 tbsp sunflower oil

To serve
small handful of chopped cilantro
   leaves
wild rice

1 Finely chop half the pineapple chunks and add to a shallow dish along with the soy, ginger, garlic, lime juice and zest, and allspice.

2 Cut a couple of slashes into each chicken thigh, add to the dish, and coat in the mix. Cover and leave to marinate for 1 hour in the fridge.

3 Preheat the oven to 400°F (200°C). Line a high-sided roasting pan with parchment paper. Spread the chicken out in the pan, and scrape over any remaining marinade. Add the remaining pineapple chunks, bell pepper, and thyme, and drizzle with oil. Bake for 40–45 minutes.

4 Scatter with chopped cilantro and serve with wild rice.

PURPLE SKY COOKIES

Blackberry purée mixed into the batter gives these irresistible cookies a purple glow that reflects the Pandoran night skies. To make these vegan, replace the butter with dairy-free baking spread and use dark chocolate chips instead of white.

Makes 12

Prep 10 mins plus chilling
Cook 10 mins

3½oz (100g) frozen blackberries, defrosted
5 tbsp (75g) unsalted butter
½ cup (100g) granulated sugar
1 tsp vanilla extract
1¼ cups (185g) all-purpose flour
½ tsp baking powder
pinch of sea salt
½ cup (70g) white chocolate chips

1 Push the blackberries through a sieve and discard any seeds. In a bowl, cream together the butter and sugar with an electric whisk until light and fluffy. Add the blackberry purée and vanilla extract, and beat well to combine.

2 Sift the flour, baking powder, and salt over the blackberry mixture and stir by hand to make a sticky dough. Fold in the chocolate chips, reserving a quarter to add to the cookies after baking—the dough will be very soft. Cover and chill in the fridge for at least 30 minutes.

3 Preheat the oven to 400ºF (200ºC). Line a baking sheet with parchment paper.

4 Roll 12 tablespoonfuls of the dough into walnut-sized balls and place them onto the prepared baking sheet, pressing down slightly on each cookie.

5 Bake for 8–10 minutes or until the edges are set. Cool on the baking sheet for a few minutes, then press the remaining chocolate chips into the cookies. Transfer to a wire rack to cool completely.

INDEX

159

Senior Editor Alastair Dougall
Project Art Editor Jon Hall
Proofreader Kayla Dugger
Production Editor Siu Yin Chan
Senior Production Controller Mary Slater
Managing Editor Emma Grange
Managing Art Editor Vicky Short
Publishing Director Mark Searle

Produced for DK by XAB Design
www.xabdesign.com

Creative Director Nigel Wright
Designers Nigel Wright, Jan Browne
Managing Editor Katie Hardwicke
Photography Nigel Wright
Food Stylist Ellie Jarvis
Prop Stylist Jan Browne

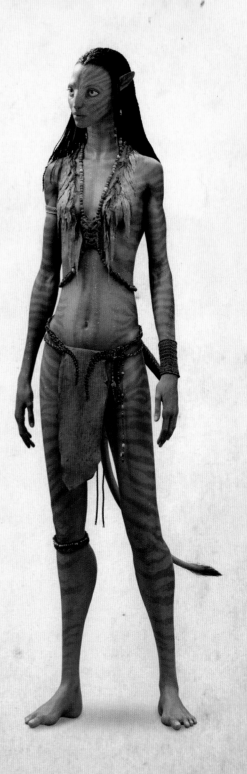

First American Edition, 2023
Published in the United States by DK Publishing
1745 Broadway, 20th Floor, New York, NY 10019

Page design copyright © 2023 Dorling Kindersley Limited
DK, a Division of Penguin Random House LLC
23 24 25 26 10 9 8 7 6 5 4 3 2 1
001–336794–Nov/2023

A catalog record for this book is available from the Library of Congress.
ISBN 978-0-7440-8551-8

DK books are available at special discounts when purchased
in bulk for sales promotions, premiums, fund-raising, or educational use. For details, contact:
DK Publishing Special Markets, 1745 Broadway, 20th Floor, New York, NY 10019
SpecialSales@dk.com

Printed and bound in China

www.dk.com

This book was made with Forest
Stewardship Council™ certified
paper—one small step in DK's
commitment to a sustainable future.
For more information go to
www.dk.com/our-green-pledge